SCAN THE
TO CHECK OUT OUR
OTHER BOOKS

G000122351

THE BRAIN BECOMES MORE ACTIVE IF IT IS SLEEP-DEPRIVED

· ·

WHEN SHUFFLING A PACK OF CARDS, THE NUMBER OF POSSIBLE COMBINATIONS IS LARGER THAN THE NUMBER OF STARS IN THE OBSERVABLE UNIVERSE

· ·

VIDEO GAMES HAVE BEEN FOUND TO BE MORE EFFECTIVE IN DEALING WITH DEPRESSION THAN THERAPY

THE FEAR OF LOUD NOISE
AND THE FEAR OF FALLING
ARE THE ONLY 2 FEARS
THAT WE ARE BORN WITH

THE GREAT PYRAMID OF
GIZA ACTUALLY HAS 8
SIDES RATHER THAN 4

THE BUMBLEBEE BAT IS
THE WORLD'S SMALLEST
MAMMAL

YOU CAN BUY SPAGHETTI FROM MCDONALDS IN THE PHILIPPINES

....

ANY PRIME NUMBER GREATER THAN 3 WILL ALWAYS BE A MULTIPLE OF 24 WHEN SQUARED AND SUBTRACTED BY 1

....

DOGS CANNOT SEE OR HEAR WHEN THEY ARE FIRST BORN. THE FIRST SENSE THEY DEVELOP IS TOUCH

THE BIGGER THE BRAIN OF AN ANIMAL, THE LONGER THEIR YAWN WILL BE

· ·

SIRI WAS ORIGINALLY MADE TO BE AN APP FOR BLACKBERRY AND ANDROID BEFORE BEING PURCHASED BY APPLE

· ·

NUTELLA WAS INVENTED DURING THE SECOND WORLD WAR AS A CHEAPER ALTERNATIVE TO CHOCOLATE

"THE MAILLARD REACTION" IS THE SCIENTIFIC NAME FOR TOASTING A PIECE OF BREAD

....

IT IS ESTIMATED THAT THERE ARE 30 TIMES LESS STARS IN THE MILKY WAY THAN THERE ARE TREES ON EARTH

....

A JELLYFISH WILL NOT DIE UNLESS IT IS KILLED BY AN EXTERNAL MEANS. THEY ARE CONSIDERED IMMORTAL

THERE ARE MORE LEGO FIGURES THAN THERE ARE PEOPLE ON EARTH

· ·

THE ROMAN-PERSIAN WARS ARE THE LONGEST IN HISTORY, LASTING 680 YEARS

· ·

ELVIS' ORIGINAL HAIR COLOUR WAS ACTUALLY BLONDE

OCTOPI AND SQUID
ACTUALLY HAVE BEAKS
MADE OF KERATIN

· ·

IT IS ESTIMATED THAT
AROUND 50 PERCENT OF
THE WORLD'S GOLD EVER
MINED CAME FROM A
PLATEAU IN SOUTH AFRICA

· ·

THE PHRASE "KEEP CALM
AND CARRY ON"
ORIGINATED DURING THE
SECOND WORLD WAR

TIRANA IS THE ONLY EUROPEAN CAPITAL CITY TO NOT HAVE A MCDONALDS

....

THE LARGEST JAPANESE POPULATION OUTSIDE OF JAPAN CAN BE FOUND IN BRAZIL

....

VIOLIN BOWS ARE COMMONLY MADE FROM HORSE HAIR

THE YOUNGEST POPE WAS POPE BENEDICT IX WHO WAS 11 YEARS OLD

··

THERE IS AN ISLAND CALLED "JUST ENOUGH ROOM" WHERE THERE IS JUST ENOUGH ROOM FOR A HOUSE AND A TREE

··

AMERICANS CONSIDER $2.4 MILLION AS THE AMOUNT YOU NEED IN ORDER TO BE WEALTHY

THE AVERAGE 150 POUND
HUMAN WILL BURN 114
CALORIES AN HOUR
WHILST STANDING UP

• •

ALTHOUGH GPS IN THE
USA IS FREE, IT COSTS ON
AVERAGE $2 MILLION PER
DAY WHICH IS PAID
THROUGH TAXES

• •

IN WW2, GERMANY
DROPPED MILLIONS OF
POUNDS OF COUNTERFEIT
MONEY OVER LONDON IN
AN ATTEMPT TO DESTROY
THE BRITISH ECONOMY

THE COLOUR RED
DOESN'T ACTUALLY MAKE
BULLS ANGRY AS THEY
ARE COLOUR BLIND

....

ONLY AROUND 10 PERCENT
OF THE POPULATION ARE
LEFT-HANDED, WHEREAS
65 PERCENT OF THOSE
WITH AUTISM ARE LEFT-
HANDED

....

UNTIL 2016, THE HAPPY
BIRTHDAY SONG WAS
COPYRIGHTED AND
NEEDED A LICENCE FOR
USE

DUE TO BEING HUNTED
BY A NUMBER OF
PREDATORS, MICE ONLY
LIVE FOR AROUND 6
MONTHS IN THE WILD

· ·

LETTUCE IS ACTUALLY A
MEMBER OF THE
SUNFLOWER FAMILY

· ·

A COLLECTION OF
BANANAS IS KNOWN AS A
HAND

SAINT LUCIA IS THE ONLY COUNTRY IN THE ENTIRE WORLD THAT IS NAMED AFTER A WOMAN

....

BETWEEN 1979 AND 1999, PLUTO WAS CLOSER TO THE SUN THAN NEPTUNE

....

CHINA IS ATTEMPTING TO MAKE RENEWABLE ENERGY MORE INTERESTING TO CHILDREN BY BUILDING SOLAR FARMS SHAPED LIKE PANDAS

OF ALL THE PLANETS IN OUR SOLAR SYSTEM, ONLY MERCURY AND VENUS DON'T HAVE MOONS

· ·

PEOPLE ARE SUBCONSCIOUSLY ATTRACTED TO PEOPLE WHO LOOK LIKE THEIR FAMILY MEMBERS

· ·

THE DISTINCT SMELL OF RAIN COMES FROM BACTERIA, PLANT OILS AND THE OZONE LAYER

MAGNETS WILL LOSE
THEIR MAGNETISM IF THEY
ARE HEATED UP

ON AVERAGE, 200
PEOPLE DIE ON CRUISE
SHIPS EVERY YEAR

SINCE 1955, HALF OF
NIGER'S POPULATION HAS
CONSISTENTLY BEEN
UNDER THE AGE OF 16

THE OLDEST UNOPENED
BOTTLE OF WINE IS OVER
1,600 YEARS OLD

THERE ARE MORE TORNADOES PER SQUARE MILE IN THE UK THAN ANY OTHER COUNTRY

· ·

TIMES SQUARE WAS ORIGINALLY CALLED LONGACRE SQUARE

· ·

IN SILICON VALLEY, THERE IS A STATUE OF NIKOLA TESLA THAT GIVES OFF FREE WIFI

ON THE PLANET VENUS, IT SNOWS METAL

....

TIC TACS ARE KNOWN BY THEIR NAME BECAUSE OF THE SOUND THEY MAKE WHEN THEIR CONTAINER IS SHAKEN

....

LANDLORDS ARE NOT REQUIRED TO PROVIDE A FRIDGE IN LOS ANGELES

....

MOST MALE CATS PREFER TO USE THEIR LEFT PAW, BUT FEMALE CATS PREFER TO USE THEIR RIGHT PAW

A BOLT OF LIGHTNING CAN BE UP TO 5 TIMES HOTTER THAN THE SURFACE OF THE SUN

· ·

IN SECOND GRADE, SHAKIRA WAS TOLD BY HER TEACHER THAT SHE SOUNDED LIKE A GOAT

· ·

OF THE 7 TOP GROSSING FILMS OF ALL TIME, 4 OF THEM WERE RELEASED IN 2015

THE QUIETEST ROOM IN
THE WORLD IS SO QUIET
THAT YOU CAN HEAR
YOUR OWN HEARTBEAT

· ·

GAMING-RELATED
ACCIDENTS INCREASED BY
AROUND A QUARTER
DURING THE FIRST 5
MONTHS OF POKEMON GO

· ·

STARFISH DON'T HAVE
BLOOD. THEY INSTEAD
CIRCULATE NUTRIENTS BY
USING SEAWATER

MOUNT RUSHMORE TOOK 14 YEARS TO MAKE AND COST LESS THAN $1 MILLION

· ·

GECKOS WILL EAT THEIR OWN SHEDDED SKIN IN ORDER TO PREVENT BEING LOCATED BY PREDATORS

· ·

DISNEYLAND WAS INSPIRED BY A MERRY-GO-ROUND IN GRIFFITH PARK, LOS ANGELES

VOLVO INVENTED THE SEATBELTS WE USE TODAY, BUT GAVE THE INVENTION AWAY FOR FREE DUE TO ITS IMPORTANCE TO SAFTEY

· ·

OLYMPUS MONS IS THE TALLEST MOUNTAIN IN OUR SOLAR SYSTEM AND IS 3 TIMES THE HEIGHT OF EVEREST

· ·

THE BRITISH POUND IS THE OLDEST CURRENCY STILL IN USE

THE EIFFEL TOWER GETS RE-PANTED EVERY 7 YEARS

....

A BLUE WHALE'S HEART IS THE SAME SIZE AS A VW BEETLE

....

HARRY POTTER WAS ORIGINALLY REJECTED BY 12 PUBLISHERS BEFORE FINALLY BEING ACCEPTED

....

LEECHES ARE KNOWN TO BE ATTRACTED TO GARLIC

BUBBLE WRAP WAS ORIGINALLY DESIGNED TO BE WALLPAPER

· ·

BY THE AGE OF 15, ALBERT EINSTEIN HAD ALREADY MASTERED CALCULUS

· ·

IN THE SAME WAY THAT HUMANS FIND PUPPIES AND BABIES CUTE, ELEPHANTS FIND HUMANS CUTE

THE AVERAGE AMERICAN OWNS 7 PAIRS OF BLUE JEANS

. . . .

FEEDING CURRY TO A SHEEP CAN REDUCE ITS METHANE PRODUCTION BY 40 PERCENT

. . . .

COLD SHOWERS HAVE A GREATER NUMBER OF HEALTH BENEFITS THAN WARM SHOWERS. BENEFITS INCLUDE IMPROVED CIRCULATION AND WEIGHT LOSS

IT TAKES URANUS 84 YEARS TO ORBIT THE SUN ONCE

....

A 26-SIDED SHAPE IS KNOWN AS A RHOMBICUBOCTAHEDRON

....

THE TOTAL WEIGHT OF ALL THE AIR ON EARTH IS 11 QUINTILLION POUNDS

....

THE NUMBER OF TIGERS IN CAPTIVITY IN THE UNITED STATES IS GREATER THAN THE NUMBER OF TIGERS IN THE WILD, WORLDWIDE

DURING A HUMAN CONVERSATION, EACH SPEAKER'S TURN TAKES 2 SECONDS ON AVERAGE

· ·

MONGOLIA HAS A NAVY DESPITE BEING A LANDLOCKED COUNTRY

· ·

ZEBRAS ONLY HAVE ONE TOE ON EACH FOOT

· ·

SURGEONS IN ANCIENT ROME WERE TRAINED TO BLOCK OUT THE NOISE OF HUMAN SCREAMS

MORE MACARONI CHEESE IS EATEN IN CANADA THAN ANY OTHER COUNTRY

· ·

A FEMALE OCTOPUS WILL SOMETIMES STRANGLE AND EAT THE MALE AFTER MATING

· ·

ALASKA WAS PURCHASED BY THE UNITED STATES FROM RUSSIA FOR $7.2 MILLION IN 1866. THE PURCHASE WAS MADE VIA A CHEQUE

SUDAN HAS TWICE THE
NUMBER OF PYRAMIDS
THAT EGYPT HAS

· ·

THE STATUE OF LIBERTY
WAS A GIFT FROM FRANCE
TO THE USA DURING THE
AMERICAN REVOLUTION

· ·

SNAKES CAN DETECT AN
EARTHQUAKE UP TO FIVE
DAYS BEFORE IT HAPPENS
AND FROM 75 MILES AWAY

IT IS ILLEGAL TO OWN ONLY ONE GUINEA PIG IN SWITZERLAND

....

ALASKA IS THE ONLY U.S. STATE THAT CAN BE SPELT ON ONE LINE OF A STANDARD KEYBOARD

....

SPIKEY DOG COLLARS WERE ORIGINALLY INVENTED TO PROTECT DOGS FROM WOLF ATTACKS

THE TERMS "MR" AND "MRS" ORIGINATE FROM THE WORDS MASTER AND MISTRESS

· ·

THE LAST OLYMPIC GOLD MEDALS MADE ENTIRELY OUT OF GOLD WERE GIVEN OUT IN THE 1912 OLYMPIC GAMES

· ·

HOUSTON IS THE MOST ETHNICALLY DIVERSE CITY IN THE UNITED STATES

DINOSAURS WOULD OFTEN CONSUME ROCKS TO HELP BREAK UP AND DIGEST THEIR FOOD

....

THE WORD "ROBOT" ORIGINATES FROM THE WORD "ROBOTA" WHICH TRANSLATES INTO FORCED LABOUR OR WORK

....

IN A REMOTE NORWEGIAN ISLAND CALLED SVALBARD, IT IS ILLEGAL TO DIE DUE TO PERMAFROST MAKING IT HARD TO BURY BODIES

THE REASON WE FEEL
"HANGRY" IS BECAUSE WE
STRUGGLE TO CONTROL
OUR EMOTIONS WHEN OUR
BRAINS HAVE LOW
GLUCOSE LEVELS

....

AN NYPD POLICE OFFICER
WOULD OFTEN FOLLOW
AROUND ANDRE THE
GIANT TO MAKE SURE HE
WOULDNT GET DRUNK AND
FALL ON ANYONE

....

THE FIRST TATTOO
MACHINE WAS ADAPTED
FROM AN ELECTRIC PEN

THE DRIVER'S WINDOW IS THE ONLY WINDOW THAT OPENS ON THE PRESIDENTIAL CAR

· ·

DEADPOOL'S COVER OF ITS 27TH ISSUE HOLDS THE RECORD FOR THE MOST COMIC BOOK CHARACTERS ON A COMIC COVER

· ·

THE WORD "ALMOST" IS THE LONGEST WORD IN THE ENGLISH LANGUAGE TO HAVE ALL ITS LETTERS IN ALPHABETICAL ORDER

YOUR TONSILS CAN GROW
BACK IF THERE WAS
TISSUE LEFT BEHIND WHEN
THEY WERE REMOVED

· ·

THE HUMAN EYE MOVES
50 TIMES ON AVERAGE
EVERY SINGLE SECOND

· ·

GREEN EYES ARE THE
RAREST COLOUR EYES
YOU CAN HAVE. ONLY 2
PERCENT OF THE WORLD'S
POPULATION HAVE GREEN
EYES

DANIEL RADCLIFFE'S BODY DOUBLE TRAGICALLY BECAME PARALYSED DURING FILMING FOR THE 7TH HARRY POTTER FILM

....

HONEY HAS BEEN FOUND TO BE ABLE TO PRESERVE ITEMS FOR CENTURIES

....

THE ODDS OF BEING BORN ON FEBRUARY 29TH ARE 1 IN 1461 DUE TO IT ONLY BEING A DAY EVERY 4 YEARS

IF YOU DONATE BLOOD IN SWEDEN, YOU WILL BE SENT A TEXT EVERY TIME YOUR BLOOD SAVES SOMEONE'S LIFE

. . . .

CHILDREN IN THE UNITED STATES MAKE UP 3.7 PERCENT OF CHILDREN ON EARTH, BUT HAVE 47 PERCENT OF CHILDREN'S TOYS AND BOOKS

. . . .

AROUND 25 PERCENT OF BLOOD FROM THE HEART GOES STRAIGHT TO THE KIDNEYS

COMETS ABSORB 96 PERCENT OF LIGHT THAT SHINES ON THEM

....

THE LORD OF THE RINGS: THE RETURN OF THE KING HOLDS THE RECORD FOR THE HIGHEST NUMBER OF ON-SCREEN DEATHS - 836

....

THERE IS AN ISLAND IN THE BAHAMAS THAT IS INHABITED ENTIRELY BY SWIMMING PIGS

DINOFLAGELLATES IS A PLANKTON THAT CAN REVERSE YOUR FEELING OF HOT AND COLD

. . . .

THE SHADOW OF AN ATOM IS THE SMALLEST THING THAT HAS EVER BEEN PHOTOGRAPHED

. . . .

DESPITE NOT BEING THE CLOSEST PLANET TO THE SUN, VENUS IS THE HOTTEST PLANET IN OUR SOLAR SYSTEM

IT TAKES LONGER TO DROWN IN SALTWATER THAN IT DOES IN FRESHWATER

. . . .

SWEDEN HAS 221,000 ISLANDS - MORE THAN ANY OTHER COUNTRY IN THE WORLD

. . . .

A TOTAL OF $1.5 MILLION IS SPENT ON HALLOWEEN COSTUMES IN THE UNITED STATES EVERY YEAR

THERE IS A CURSE ENGRAVED ON WILLIAM SHAKESPEARE'S GRAVE TO STOP ANYONE MOVING HIS BONES

· ·

ON VALENTINE'S DAY IN SOUTH KOREA, ONLY WOMEN GIVE GIFTS, AND MEN RECEIVE THEM

· ·

THERE ARE 1,800 THUNDERSTORMS HAPPENING ON EARTH AT ANY GIVEN TIME

BOANTHROPY IS A PSYCHOLOGICAL DISORDER IN WHICH PEOPLE BELIEVE THEY ARE A COW

· ·

THERE IS A BRITISH CHOCOLATE SCIENTIST WHO INSURED HER TASTE BUDS FOR £1 MILLION

· ·

DESPITE BEING WIDELY TRAINED FOR DOG FIGHTING, PITBULLS ARE ONE OF THE MOST AFFECTIONATE BREEDS OF DOG

OWLS HAVE FEATHERS THAT PROTRUDE OUT, ALLOWING THEM TO FLY SILENTLY DUE TO A DISRUPTION TO AIR FLOW

. . . .

THERE WERE MORE CASUALTIES IN THE BATTLE OF STALINGRAD THAN IN HIROSHIMA AND NAGASAKI COMBINED

. . . .

20 PERCENT OF ALL THE OXYGEN IN YOUR BODY IS USED BY YOUR BRAIN

THE UNITED STATES
MILITARY INCLUDES
DOLPHINS THAT ARE
TRAINED TO RESCUE LOST
NAVAL SOLDIERS

· ·

THERE ARE ESTIMATED
TO BE OVER A BILLION
TIMES MORE INSECTS ON
EARTH THAN HUMANS

· ·

SNOOP DOG GOT HIS NAME
FROM HIS MUM WHO
THOUGHT HE LOOKED LIKE
SNOOPY FROM PEANUTS

KANGAROOS CONTINUE TO GROW RIGHT UP UNTIL THE MOMENT THEY PASS AWAY

• •

IT ONLY TAKES 20 SECONDS FOR A RED BLOOD CELL TO TRAVEL AROUND THE ENTIRE HUMAN BODY

• •

SCIENTISTS STILL DON'T KNOW WHY THE STREAM OF WATER FROM A SHOWER CAUSES THE SHOWER CURTAIN TO MOVE INWARD

IT IS BELIEVED THAT TYRANNOSAURUS REXES WERE BORN WITH FEATHERS TO KEEP THEM WARM

· ·

A SNAIL CAN SLEEP FOR UP TO 3 YEARS

· ·

BEN AND JERRY'S HAVE AN ONLINE GRAVEYARD WHERE YOU CAN FIND ALL DISCONTINUED FLAVOURS AND EVEN ASK TO 'RESURRECT' A FLAVOUR YOU WANT BACK

IN THE AZTEC PERIOD, A SLAVE COULD BE PURCHASED FOR ONLY 100 COCOA BEANS

. . . .

BECAUSE BEES FLAP THEIR WINGS TO REGULATE HEAT, A BEEHIVE IS OFTEN THE SAME TEMPERATURE AS THE HUMAN BODY

. . . .

THE LACOSTE LOGO WAS THE FIRST DESIGNER LOGO EVER MADE

THE LENGTH OF A DAY ON
NEPTUNE IS 16 HOURS 6
MINUTES AND 36 SECONDS

· ·

DOGS WHO HAVE POINTED
FACES, SUCH AS THOSE
WITH SNOUTS, TEND TO
LIVE LONGER THAN THOSE
WITH FLAT FACES

· ·

ON AVERAGE, THE HUMAN
HEART WILL BEAT 3.6
MILLION TIMES EVERY
SINGLE YEAR. IF YOU LIVE
UNTIL 80, IT WILL BEAT
288 MILLION TIMES IN
YOUR LIFE

IT TAKES OVER 800 BEES TO PRODUCE A STANDARD JAR OF HONEY

· ·

7.8 PERCENT OF AMERICAN ADULTS BELIEVE THAT CHOCOLATE MILK COMES FROM BROWN COWS

· ·

IT TAKES JUPITER 11.86 EARTH YEARS TO TRAVEL AROUND THE SUN. THIS MEANS THAT A YEAR ON JUPITER IS 4,328 DAYS

IT IS ESTIMATED THAT
AROUND 15 PERCENT OF
ALL ACCOUNTS ON
TWITTER ARE
CONTROLLED BY BOTS

....

JUST OVER HALF OF THE
LONDON UNDERGROUND IS
ACTUALLY BELOW THE
SURFACE

....

THERE ARE NEARLY TWICE
AS MANY KANGAROOS IN
AUSTRALIA AS THERE ARE
HUMANS

IT IS ESTIMATED THAT AROUND 15 PERCENT OF IPHONE USERS USE DEVICES THAT HAVE A BROKEN SCREEN

. . . .

A BROKEN HEART ISN'T JUST A FIGURE OF SPEECH. ELEPHANTS CAN DIE OF A BROKEN HEART IF THEIR MATE DIES

. . . .

MAGEIROCOPHOBIA IS ANOTHER NAME FOR THE FEAR OF COOKING

RATS ARE TRAINED TO SNIFF OUT LANDMINES IN CAMBODIA. THEY CAN DO THE SAME JOB AS HUMANS IN A SIGNIFICANTLY QUICKER TIME

· ·

PAUL MCCARTNEY WAS ONLY PAID £1 FOR HIS PERFORMANCE AT THE 2012 OLYMPICS OPENING CEREMONY

· ·

MORE THAN 1.9 BILLION SERVINGS OF COCA COLA ARE CONSUMED EVERY DAY

SUNFLOWERS ARE THOUGHT TO BE ABLE TO CLEAN RADIOACTIVE SOIL

. . . .

LOVE IS THE MOST USED HASHTAG ON INSTAGRAM

. . . .

YOUR FOOT IS THE SAME LENGTH AS THE DISTANCE FROM YOUR ELBOW TO YOUR WRIST

IN ANCIENT GREECE, THROWING AN APPLE AT A WOMAN WAS A WAY OF DECLARING YOUR LOVE FOR THEM

• •

PEOPLE BLINK AROUND 3 TIMES LESS WHEN THEY USE A COMPUTER COMPARED TO NOT USING A COMPUTER

• •

THE SKIPPER BUTTERFLY CAN FLY FASTER THAN A HORSE CAN RUN

DESPITE ITS SIZE, THE EMPIRE STATE BUILDING ONLY TOOK 410 DAYS TO BUILD

· ·

THE PLANET NEPTUNE WAS NOT DISCOVERED THROUGH A TELESCOPE BUT INSTEAD BY MATHEMATICAL PREDICTIONS

· ·

FOXES HAVE WHISKERS ON THEIR LEGS TO HELP THEM FIND THEIR WAY AROUND IN THE DARK

VOLKSWAGEN OWNS BENTLEY, BUGATTI, LAMBORGHINI, AUDI AND PORSCHE

· ·

ON AVERAGE, PEOPLE IN FRANCE SLEEP LONGER THAN ANY OTHER COUNTRY IN THE DEVELOPED WORLD

· ·

AKON IS THE NUMBER 1 SELLING ARTIST FOR RINGTONES IN THE WORLD

WHEN YOU REMEMBER AN EVENT OF THE PAST, YOU ARE ACTUALLY REMEMBERING THE LAST TIME YOU REMEMBERED IT, NOT THE EVENT ITSELF

THE WORD OXYMORON IS IN FACT AN OXYMORON ITSELF AS OXY MEANS SHARP AND MORON MEANS STUPID

8 TREES ARE REQUIRED TO PRODUCE ENOUGH OXYGEN FOR 1 PERSON FOR A YEAR

TAKING A SINGLE STEP WHEN WALKING USES 200 MUSCLES IN YOUR BODY

....

THE NAME OF THE ONLINE CLOTHING STORE ASOS IS AN ACRONYM FOR 'AS SEEN ON SCREEN'

....

THERE ARE NATURALLY OCCURRING CHEMICALS IN COCOA BEANS THAT FIGHT HARMFUL BACTERIA IN YOUR MOUTH, MEANING COCOA CAN BE USED TO PREVENT TOOTH DECAY

NASA STANDS FOR "NATIONAL AERONAUTICS AND SPACE ADMINISTRATION"

· ·

THE AGE OF THE UNIVERSE IS ESTIMATED TO BE 13.7 BILLION YEARS OLD

· ·

BECAUSE IT IS KNOWN TO BOOST YOUR METABOLISM, DRINKING GREEN TEA BEFORE BED CAN HELP YOU BURN MORE CALORIES WHILE YOU SLEEP

DISNEY WORLD IS THE SECOND LARGEST PURCHASER OF EXPLOSIVES IN THE UNITED STATES, BEHIND ONLY THE COUNTRY'S DEFENCE DEPARTMENT

COCA COLA DEVELOPED SPRITE TO DIRECTLY COMPETE WITH 7-UP

AROUND 70 PERCENT OF PEOPLE TILT THEIR HEAD TO THE RIGHT WHEN KISSING SOMEONE

IF YOU HAVE A TICKLY THROAT, SCRATCHING YOUR EAR CAN SOMETIMES CAUSE THE SENSATION TO GO AWAY

· ·

THERE ARE MORE STARS IN SPACE THAN THERE ARE GRAINS OF SAND ON PLANET EARTH

· ·

ROUGHLY 70 PERCENT OF THE EARTH IS COVERED BY WATER, BUT 97 PERCENT OF THIS IS SALTWATER

HUMANS CANNOT WALK IN A STRAIGHT LINE WITHOUT BEING ABLE TO SEE

....

DESPITE BEING THE SECOND LARGEST PLANET IN OUR SOLAR SYSTEM, SATURN IS THE LIGHTEST. THIS IS BECAUSE IT IS A GAS GIANT

....

VICTORIA'S SECRET WAS ORIGINALLY SUPPOSED TO BE A STORE FOR MEN TO SHOP FOR THEIR FEMALE PARTNERS WITHOUT FEELING EMBARRASSED

INTENTIONALLY FARTING ON A CALIFORNIAN PRISON GUARD CAN GET YOU AN ADDITIONAL 11 YEARS IN PRISON

· ·

BILL GATES' HOUSE WAS DESIGNED USING AN APPLE COMPUTER

· ·

A SWAN HAS MORE THAN 25,000 FEATHERS ON ITS BODY

THERE ARE MORE SELFIE-RELATED DEATHS EVERY YEAR THAN SHARK-RELATED DEATHS

....

MALE CATS ARE CALLED TOMS AND FEMALE CATS ARE CALLED MOLLIES

....

BUTTERFLIES DON'T HAVE NORMAL SKELETONS. THEY HAVE SOMETHING CALLED AN EXOSKELETON WHICH LIES ON THE OUTSIDE OF THEIR BODY

TUTANKHAMUN'S PARENTS WERE BROTHER AND SISTER

....

A BOTTLE OF COCA COLA CAN DISSOLVE A HUMAN NAIL IN JUST 4 DAYS

....

ALL OF THE SIMPSONS CHARACTERS HAVE 4 FINGERS APART FROM ONE. THE 'GOD' IN THE SHOW HAS 5 FINGERS AND IS THE ONLY ONE THAT DOES

IN ORDER FOR A GIRAFFE TO PUMP ENOUGH BLOOD TO ITS HEAD, ITS HEART NEEDS TO BEAT TWICE AS HARD AS A COW'S HEART

· ·

THE PINKY PROMISE GOT ITS NAME FROM THE IDEA THAT WHOEVER BROKE THE PROMISE WOULD HAVE THEIR PINKY FINGER CUT OFF

· ·

NO TWO GIRAFFES HAVE THE SAME PATTERN

Printed in Great Britain
by Amazon

11706666R00038